Get It Together!

Organize Your Space and Feel Better About Your Life!

Room-by-Room, practical advice on getting your house clean, organized and ready for the future!

Kathleen Abbott

Copyright © 2011 by Kathleen Abbott

All rights reserved. Without limiting the rights under copyright reserved above, no part of this publication may be reproduced, stored in or introduced into a retrieval system, or transmitted, in any form or by any means (electronic, mechanical, photocopying, recording or otherwise), without the prior written permission of both the copyright owner and the above publisher of this book.

This publication is designed to provide accurate and authoritative information in regard to the subject matter covered. It is sold with the understanding that the publisher is not engaged in rendering legal, accounting, or other professional service. If legal advice or other expert assistance is required, the services of a competent professional person should be sought.— *From a Declaration of Principles Jointly Adopted by a Committee of the American Bar Association and a Committee of Publishers and Associations*

Printed in the United States of America

ISBN 978-1-105-00399-8

Table of Contents

Welcome	7
Step-by-Step	11
Room-by-Room	13
Make-a-Plan	15
Containers and Organizers	17
Cleaning Tools and Supplies	19
Finale to the Organization	21
Kitchen	23
Dining Room	29
Living Room/Family Room	31
Hall Closet	33
Laundry Room	35
Bedroom	37
Bathroom/Linen Closet	41

Playroom	47
Office	51
Storage Room	55
Garage/Shed	59
Conclusion	63
Where to buy Websites	65

Welcome!

I know you may seem overwhelmed with everything in your life. I know I did.

But here's a secret: If you get your personal space cleared and in order, then you will be amazed at how much better you will feel. Your world – and your life! -will have some order to it.

With an orderly home things are easier to find, and things get done in a timely manner. It s true for me: I feel more productive and my life seems less hectic if there is a place for everything and everything is in its place. I feel out of sorts when things are disorganized and my space is a mess. I have no motivation to do anything!

It simplifies your life, too; when you keep things in order, you don't hold onto things that you do not use thus: less clutter.

In this book, I hope that I can give you some good ideas on how to get your home in order, relieving your anxieties and tensions in the process. You will get ideas on new ways to do things, and you may even think of ways to get even more organized on

your own. My ideas aren't the only ones. Hopefully they will be just a starting point; to get your thinking of ways you could do it to fit your own unique situation.

It wasn't easy to gain this insight. It only began for me after I suddenly, found myself a single Mom.

At first, I was devastated. I lost all motivation to do anything. I gained weight. The house didn't really seem to take any priority in my life. "Why keep it clean and neat?" I asked myself. My five- and six-year-olds didn't notice the mess, so why should I care?

After too long a time, I came to realize that I couldn't live like that any longer. I decided to get things back in order. In the past, people had always commented on how organized and neat I was. I realized that was important to me, so I got to work... and I was amazed at how I began to feel. When I got my home in order, everything started to fall into place.

I found out I wasn't the only one who felt this way. I have a friend whose husband passed away recently, when her son was only a few months old. Although her situation was very different from mine—she was dealing with other issues, of course her house was a mess too. It looked good on the surface, but her closets, drawers and cupboards were a mess. I went over one weekend and helped her out... and she was thrilled at what I did and how I got her organized. You can do the same! You

may not have gone through a divorce or a death in the family, but whatever has happened in your life to make you feel helpless and unmotivated doing the smallest things can help you get back on track. I know from personal experience that an un-kept home will pull you down.

(The same is true of an un-kept body, but I'm not going to try and give you advice on how to keep yourself up physically . . . although I know that exercise and a healthy diet make the world of difference in how you feel!)

It can be done! It just takes the determination to do it.

But how do you get started? Well, let me give you a few ideas . . .

Step-by-Step

This is the first and most important thing: take it one step at a time.

If you try and do it all at once, you will just become overwhelmed – and you're already overwhelmed enough as it is!

So take it step-by-step. Go room-by-room, and even within the room, start with one area and then work your way through it all.

It doesn't have to happen overnight, either. Or even in one weekend. Set your own schedule. Maybe you can do, say, one room a month. You can pick a day or a weekend that can be used as your cleaning/organization time. You can even schedule specific days or evenings around the holidays to do that 'special' work – a time in December to put up the decorations and a time in January to put them away. This will make the time more enjoyable for you and your family.

If you can get into the habit of doing a little bit at a time, and setting aside a specific time to do it then your home will be more organized and it will become easier for everyone.

And keep in mind that this is a never ending job . . . but the more you keep yourself organized the more enjoyable it will be to be at home to rest or entertain.

Remember: *You have to take baby steps before you can run the marathon.*

Room-by-Room

Let's take this one room at a time. It will make things easier.

- Kitchen: Day:_____ Month:_____
- Dining Room   Day:_____ Month:_____
- Living Room   Day:_____ Month:_____
- Family Room   Day:_____ Month:_____
- Hall Closet(s) Day:_____ Month:_____
- Laundry Room Day:_____ Month:_____
- Bedroom   Day:_____ Month:_____
- Bathroom/
  Linen Closet   Day:_____ Month:_____
- Playroom   Day:_____ Month:_____
- Office   Day:_____ Month:_____
- Storage Room Day:_____ Month:_____
- Garage   Day:_____ Month:_____

Make-a-Plan

Once you've made the decision to pull it together, it's tempting to dive right in. But take a moment first and make a plan.

> First: Take a thorough look at what you will need to get your chosen area into shape. What will be needed to organize those particular drawers, closets, and cupboards? Use the following pages to Make-A-Plan every time you take on a new room.
>
> Second: Go to the stores and purchase whatever items are need.
>
> Third: Clear the area out and clean it up.

And finally ... Keep it up!

- Visit my blog for even more information and ideas!
- Check out the links to stores where you can buy great organizing gadgets and tools. Check out **page 65** for the details!

Containers and Organizers

Room: _____

What containers or organizers will you need?

   Cardboard boxes:

      How Many? _____

      Size(s): _____

   "Banker's boxes" (stackable, with lids)

      How Many? _____

      Size(s): _____

   Plastic boxes:

      How Many? _____

      Size(s): _____

   Baskets:

      How Many? _____

      Size(s): _____

   Canisters of Cans:

      How Many? _____

      Size(s): _____

- Drawer Dividers:

    How Many? _____

    Size(s): _____

- Shelving: (describe): _____

    Items needed: _____

- Closets:

    Hangers: _____

    Door hooks: _____

    Other Items: _____

Cleaning Tools and Supplies

Room: _____

- Broom
- Mop
- Brush

    Soft or Wire? _____

    Size (s)? _____

- Vacuum Cleaner
- Buckets
- Cleaning Rags
- Scrubbing pads
- Sponges
- Paper Towels
- Glass/Window cleaner
- Chrome cleaner
- Sink/Toilet cleaner
- Wall/Surface cleaner
- Others: _____

Finale to the Organization

After you clean and straighten out the cupboards, drawers, and closets in the area, I would suggest giving it a good cleaning.

- Wipe down the door and clean off any fingerprints on the doorways or walls.
- Wash the walls, pictures, and light fixtures.
- Give the windows a thorough washing and pull and wash the window screens.
- Pull all the furniture away from the walls and vacuum or sweep.
- Thoroughly wash the floor and/or baseboards. If you have a wood floor, give it shine.
- Pull all the cushions off the couch and chairs and vacuum in the underside then flip the cushions and fluff the pillows.
- Put the furniture back. Maybe you could take this time to rearrange the furniture and give it a new look.
- Remove any knickknacks that you have on the tables and give them a good cleaning by rinsing, dusting and/or polishing.
- Polish your wood furniture with wood oil, including the wooden legs of the furniture.
- Clean up the plants by racking up the dirt and snipping all the dead, dry leaves.

- Dust off the leaves to the plants. You can use a feather duster or you may need to dampen a cloth and shine them up. (Another way to give them a good shine is by putting just a dot of mayonnaise and on a slightly damp rag and applying it to the leaf. This will give it a good shine and make it look beautiful.)
- Dust, wipe down the counter/dresser tops.
- Make the beds and fluff the pillows.

Now you have a well organized and clean area. You can then move onto your next room.

What I also do is place a laundry basket in the same area, by the back door, in the laundry room, garage, basement or wherever you think is right to have it noticeable but still out of the main walkway. What I do with this is anything I find laying around goes in this basket. This keeps the house in order and at the end of the day you put the things where they need to go. Unfortunately, this is a never-ending job but the more you keep yourself organized the more enjoyable it will be to live in the home you love.

Okay now that you're ready - let's get started!

Kitchen

The kitchen is probably the most complicated room in your house. There are so many items and so many things to put away. So give it some special thought during the planning phase. Do you need to purchase any silverware organizers, spice racks, canisters, and containers of any kind? Do you really need and use all the gadgets, spices, cans and containers you have acquired over the years? This is also the room that can require different kinds of cleaning materials: sink scrubbers like Comet, floor cleaners or waxes, tile cleaners, oven cleaners. And even special cleaners for fixtures and stovetops. Get it together!

And once you're ready . . .

Step #1

Start with the utensils, cooking tools and dining ware. Empty out all of the cupboards and drawers. Another suggestion is to do the drawers, top cupboards, bottom cupboard, pantry and refrigerator separately. Otherwise if it's all out at the same time this can be a nightmare. Try and be somewhat organized from the beginning, by placing all similar items together in the same area, like the kitchen table, the countertop, or the floor.

Now do the same with the food items not in your refrigerator. Group the spices, canned goods, baking mixes, etc.

Step #2

Clean the inside and outside of the drawers and cabinets with a soapy cloth.

Step #3

Take a look at the items you have out. Do you still use these items? If not - start a pile for the trash or for donations or for a possible yard sale. Also are some of these items seasonal? Are they summer or holiday dishes and decorations? If so, you could store them in a (labeled) container and put them in a closet, attic or the basement.

Move to the food items. When was the last time you used that particular sauce or spice? Check the expiration date, including the spices. Most lose effectiveness after a relatively short time, so saving them isn't necessary. If you haven't used any of these packages, spices, mixes, or materials in the last six months and if you don't have definite plans to use them in the next six, and then throw them away. Be ruthless.

Step #4

Start to place the items back into the cupboards ... but first:

Look at the space you have to work with, and try not to put things back where they used to be without thinking it through. Is the 'old' space really the right space? Should you get stacking accessories or a 'Lazy Susan' to use in a particular space? Should you put the dishes in one cupboard and the food in another? If you take a long, hard look, you will be able to see the space you have to work with and what is the best for you. Here are a few specific suggestions:

Dishes: Organize them by size and use: all the dinner plates, salad plates, bowls, mugs, cups and saucers. They should be stacked on top of one another.

Glassware: Organize the glasses not on size or style, but on how often you use them. If you use your milk and juice glasses daily, but your wine glasses and brandy sniffers only occasionally, then milk and juice should be easily within reach when you open the cupboard. The others can be up high or in the back.

Cookware: Put the pots and pans in a cupboard close to the oven. Arrange them like the glassware: put the ones you use the most in the front and the ones used occasionally in the back. The baking items should be put in their own cupboard.

Appliances: When was the last time you used that bread maker? Look at all the items you own – all of them! And if you have not used it in a year, then get it out of your space. You can store it where you stored the Holiday dishes, or if you don't think it will be of use to you any longer, put it in the "donation" or "yard sale" pile.

Cleaning Supplies: Remember that many of your cleaning supplies are corrosive and even toxic if spilled, accidentally mixed, or swallowed. Children and pets are especially vulnerable. But so are normally careful adults. So storing them in easily accessible areas like under the sink probably isn't a good idea. I have found that putting them in the cupboard above the refrigerator works very well. I did this when my girls were younger, when they were crawling around and getting into everything. This way the poisonous items were out of reach and I did not have to worry about them – or anyone else.

Refrigerator: Do the same thing you did with the cupboards. Empty out every shelf and drawer and look at what you have. Are there jars way in the back that you can't even remember buying? Then throw it out.

Look at the expiration dates on everything. Consolidate duplicates (you must have two half-used jars of pickles. Everyone does.) Combine them, save some space, and simplify your life.

Here are a few specific hints:

- Fruits and veggies don't have to be loose in the drawers. I have found that when I cut a piece out of the green pepper I put it in a plastic container, it stays crisp for more than a week (the 6.5"x 4.5"x 2.5" lunch meat containers are the perfect size for this). It's great to store the food items in these containers. They lock in the freshness and they store in the refrigerator very easily. Obviously, each refrigerator's layout is different, so look carefully at what you have and arrange storage in a way that is best for you.

- Meats and cheese in the meat drawer.

- Condiments in the door (not all over the place).

- Juice and milk can stay on the taller shelves.

- Leftovers on the bottom, but at the front. Leftovers pushed to the back of the fridge will be forgotten until they go bad.

In the freezer, I use big plastic tubs the size of shoe boxes. I put the meat, seafood, vegetables, desserts, breakfast foods all in their own tubs, so even the freezer is organized. (You can find the best places to purchase these tubs in the Where to Buy web site list at the back of this book.)

It's easy for your fridge to get disorganized all over

again, so make a habit of straightening the arrangement each time you go grocery shopping. This way, you will know what you need and it will also get rid of old food products. Keep a magnetic shopping pad on the fridge, and every time you use the last of something (or think of something you need to pick up for later), make a note right then and there.

Pantry: If you have a pantry, or even a cabinet that can become one, use it. I don't have a lot of extra space to keep food in my own place, but I do have a pantry closet where I keep the dry food on one shelf and all the condiments on another. This is another good place to keep a shopping list: when I take something out of the pantry and put it in the fridge (or use it), the list is right there to update, before I've used my 'back-up.'

There is nothing worse than getting all set to have BBQ chicken to find out your out of BBQ sauce. This kind of planning cuts down on duplication too: nobody needs to wind up with 5 jars of black olives. (Keep just one list though, either on the fridge or in the pantry).

Drawers: Drawers are a great way to keep items separate (silverware in one drawer, serving ladles and spoons in another), napkins and linens in another. But let's face it, every kitchen has a junk drawer, no matter how organized you might be. Don't worry. Enjoy it. (But keep it to just one!). Also: I have found dividers can help drawers do double-duty. There are many options at places like Target, Meijer's, or the Dollar Store.

Dining Room

An easy room! Really, the only thing to organize in the dining room is the hutch or buffet.

Empty out the hutch or buffet and place all the items on the table (which you cover of course to eliminate scratching). Look at the items you have and ask yourself if you actually use these items.

If you're like me, you'll realize that most of these special pieces of china or glassware are only used during the Holidays or other special occasion, and if you have the space, this is a fine place to keep those special items. But don't make it a general catch-all for old bowling trophies, diplomas or anything else you have nowhere else to store. So if you really want to keep or use those items, find a spot for them. If not... out they go.

Clean out the drawers and shelves of the hutch, and be stern with yourself about what belongs here:

- Fine China
- Silver
- Linens
- Candles, napkin rings, and other items for a formal dinner.

These are the only things that need be in this area.

Living Room/Family Room

All homes are different. Some have a formal living room and a family room plus a play room while some use the basement as their family room plus play area. Whatever your situation, I will give suggestions and you do what best suits your needs.

I try not to store anything in the formal living room. This is your living room that you use to sit back and relax.

The family room is used to relax and have fun in. I'm sure you have the T.V., DVD, Stereo System and all the games in this room so might I suggest that you store all the same things together, such as the DVD, CD, Wii, Board games. Again each home is different and you know what you have to work with but if you keep the items that are alike in the same container, shelf or closet then they are easier to find and keep track of.

This is a room that you will relax in so try and keep it somewhat organized. It's hard to relax in a room that's a mess. I know that many family rooms are also play areas which means that there are a lot of toys around. One suggestion that I have for you is to purchase a screened room divider, you can place the play area behind it so you don't have to look at the mess the kids made while you are trying to relax and watch TV.

You could be real creative and go to a hardware store and purchase the unfinished piece and have your children do a creation of their own.

Again, give the room a good cleaning after you have organized your space.

Hall Closet

You may have more than one hall closet, so let's discuss many different ideas you can use -- whatever best fits your situation.

The closet seems to be a catch all-spot. Over the years, I have used cloth or plastic baskets to store just about everything, including:

- Candles & holders
- Vacuum cleaner bags
- Chair covers
- Telephone books
- Outlet cords
- Camcorders, cameras, film and tapes
- Extra dishcloths and placemats
- Hats, scarves, and gloves
- Umbrellas

... and that's barely the beginning.

You can put all these items in containers and store them on the shelves of your closet. The baskets will hide the items and make the closet much neater and more organized.

I like to purchase wooden hangers for coats. Again, make sure they are all in the same style, and buy ones that are sturdy enough to hang your heavy coats on. You could have a larger basket sitting on the floor to hold the boots, or like most people you could store your vacuum in the hall closet (where else do find a place to store it?).

Here's another suggestion: find a cheap durable fixture designed to hold the batteries of different size and voltage; different styles are available at most hardware stores. Hang this on the side wall of the closet; this way you will always know where the batteries are and you will also be able to see when you are running low. You can hang the flash light there too, so you can also know where it is when it's needed.

I know you can't fit all of these things in one closet (well, you could ... but then it would be a mess and we d be right back where we started!), and you may have some of these items stored in other spots already. But these are suggestions for what and how things could be stored easily, neatly, and inexpensively and in a area where you can find them when you really need them.

Laundry Room

I have found it useful to have a shelf above the top of the washer and dryer. You can purchase a white piece of wood and the brackets to hold it from Lowes, Home Depot or any other hardware type of store. You can make the shelf safer and easier to clean by covering the top with drawer liner. You can purchase a roll at almost any one of the stores. It works very nicely because it is the same width, and all you need to do is roll it on. This stops the things from sliding on the shelf, and makes it easy to wipe up things that spill. Even better, when it gets real nasty replace it and it will look much nicer.

That space above the washing machine is an ideal place to store detergent, fabric softener, stain remover and all those other products that come in large bottles that are designed to lie on their sides for easier dispensing. You can keep your sewing kit there, too, along with a plastic shoe box or a small basket to hold the one sock that always seems to lose its match (it should show up sooner or later... and if not, your kids can make a sock puppet!).

You may also have space to put a cupboard above the shelf, or to add another shelf. In this area you can store a backup bottle of detergent and softeners. You can also store bleaches, distilled water (for the Iron), clothes pins, washer bags for you fine silks, fabric softener sheets, light bulbs and whatever else you have that is used for the laundry and repair.

If you have a cabinet under your sink or space under the washtub with or without a cabinet, here you can store your buckets' You can also get a plastic bin at one of the stores and store the rags in there.

Another suggestion that I have is to take a bucket and put in the bucket the glass cleaner, soft scrub (or the tile sink cleaner you use), toilet brush, Pine Sol or any room deodorizer you use, furniture polish, and a few rags. This way you have your cleaning materials all set to go and you can go from room to room and this will make the process of cleaning a bit smoother.

When you are organized in this room, now it's time to give it a good cleaning, Pull the washer and dryer away from the wall and wash the floor and give the appliances a good wash also. Clean out the lint catcher and run a cup of vinegar threw the washer with nothing in it.

Now let's move on to the next room...

Bedroom

Take a look at your closet and drawers first. Make your plan. And remember that there are many very good 'closet organizer' systems that can help you gain additional storage space and keep things neat. Do some research and make some decisions before you begin. You may need to go and purchase some things before you get started. Then get to work:

Closet: Empty out the closet placing the items on the bed, floor and dresser tops. Wipe it out and/or vacuum the inside.

Hangers: I don t know what your closet looks like -- everyone is different -- but if it has one rack to hang clothes, then you should seriously consider purchasing a devise which will allow you to install a hanging rail which hangs below the first. This way you have double the hanging space. You can hang tops and blouses on one while skirts and pants on the other. You can leave a section for longer hanging items such as dresses, long skirts and long jackets. I like to use the same kind of hangers such as plastic ones that you can purchase almost anywhere. When they all match then this does make the closet look neater and more organized.

Belts: I have also found that a belt hanger saves room. Hang the ones you wear frequently in the front.

Shoes: Use clear shoe boxes so that you can see what's inside; they are also easy to stack on top of one and other. Here, too, make an effort to store the shoes based on how they are used. The dress and seasonal ones can go to the back or the bottom, and the ones you use more frequently should stay in the front or on top.

Purses: Hang purses on the wall or stack them on a shelf, again in the order of use.

As you are placing the items back in the closet, look at what you have. Do the items still fit? Are they in style? And when was the last time it was worn? Clothes are easy to hand off or give away or even sell. Do it.

Dresser drawers: Look at the space you have and what goes into the drawers. Again, put away only the things that you wear regularly - or at all.

Dividers: Use drawer dividers to give more space to store your items.

Underwear: You can place undergarments all in the same drawer, with the brazier/undershirts and the panties/boxers in the same drawer, and still not have them mix together.

Socks: socks, sweat socks, nylons.

Separate drawers: swim wear, sleepwear, scarves, workout clothing, and any other articles of clothing you wear regularly.

Nightstand drawers: Don't let this become another junk drawer! Make sure you limit the drawer contents to truly useful or important things, such as a remote control, handkerchief, book, rosary or anything else that you use when you are in bed for the night. And nothing else!

Jewelry Box: Empty it out and look at what you have. Is any of it mismatched, incomplete, or damaged? Can you sell the gold that you no longer use? Is the style out-dated? Jewelry is just like any other item of clothing: look at it carefully, assess its importance or necessity, then keep, toss, give away, or sell.

Bathroom/Linen Closet

No room in the house seems to acquire 'stuff' as much as the bathroom. So make your plan, gather your tools, and prepare for a thorough 'sorting.' Empty out every cupboard, shelf, and cabinet and give every surface a good cleaning. Make some practical decisions about what you need and use, what s out-of-date, and what you can get rid of.

Shelves of the linen closet:

Towels: Fold the towels into consistent sizes and stack them on top of each other as you reshelf them. Fold and stack the bath, hand and wash cloths separately; don't fold them all differently and have the towels mixed with the washcloths and then shove them on the shelf.

Sheets: Do the same for your bed sheets on a different shelf.

Toiletries and medicines: Place all your medicines and frequently use toiletries on the shelf in the middle, at eye level. If you don't already have a small shelf or rack that you can hang on the door, consider buying one. This can hold many items that you use frequently and they are easier to get to. Again look at what you have to work with.

The joy of baskets. Personally, I like to use little baskets to store these items.

- Tools for nail care
- Pain relief medicines
- Make-up
- Hair care
- Band aids, gauze wraps

Each 'category' has its own basket in the appropriate size. Then larger items shampoo, hair spray, mouthwash, etc. can go on the shelf.

Medicine Cabinets: Tooth paste goes on the bottom shelf.
Many of the smaller items you need to keep could go into butter tubs or other similar small containers:

- Aspirin
- Eye drops
- Dental floss
- Tweezers
- Nail clipper and other small items

Larger bottles and vials that can stand on their own on the top shelf:

- Mouth wash
- Shampoo
- Night cream and day cream

Drawers: Shallow top drawers just below the counter-tops can also hold:
- Tooth paste
- Dental floss
- Night cream, and day cream

Another drawer can hold:
- Cotton balls
- Q-tips
- Female products

If there is another drawer it can hold the travel toiletry cases.

Make-up: I know women, we keep everything from the samples that we get in the mail to the tiny vials of shadow in a color that will go with the outfit we are wearing on a great night out. But often these individual items get used once (or not at all), and then just sit in a drawer and take up room. It is hard, but now is the time to get rid of these lovely little things you just don't use. If you must, use up the samples first, and from now on every time you get a sample in the mail or from the makeup counter, use it or dispose of it right away Then your make-up drawer or basket can do what it's designed to do: hold only items that you actually use.

Shower: if you don't already have one, get a stylish rack that can hang from the shower head, or specially made baskets that stick to the shower wall (Bed Bath and Beyond is a wonderful place!). This can hold:

- Shampoo
- Cream rinse
- Body wash
- Facial cleansers
- Razors and any other items you need in a shower.

Avoid balancing them on tiny soap dishes or in hard-to-clean corners.

Once again, how often you use a given item should determine where it goes. There really is enough space available in most bathroom vanities and cabinets; it s more a matter of planning and maintenance than spending a lot on new gadgets or storage space, and don't neglect those lower shelves. Most bathrooms have some larger, lower cabinets that are perfect for those larger appliances you don't need to have right at hand – humidifiers, massagers, and the like.

Every bathroom is different, so you need to take a look at what you have and decide what will work best for you. And I ll say again: if you empty out the area and see what you have to work with, then go through what was in the cupboards and cabinets and dispose of what you no longer need, putting things back – in a together way – will go very smoothly.

Playroom

You don't have to spend a fortune on fancy, specially made t o y " bins" for your kids. You can use every day, clear storage container, holiday-themed containers (that are on sale after the holiday is over at great discounts!), laundry baskets, or plastic drawers. Whatever is cheap and at hand is fine. Most important, be sure to label the tubs with what's inside, even if the tubs are clear. And of course, put the toys that are similar in the same tub.

- American Girl dolls
- Build-A-Bears
- Baby dolls
- GI Joes
- Puppets,
- Barbies
- Legos
- Building blocks
- Tinker-toys, etc.

For the dolls and their things: I especially like using the clear plastic drawers to store the doll things - one drawer for the dolls and another one for the clothing. These drawers stack on top of one another, which save space, and if you have a doll house they can be double convenience. You can also add drawers as needed for the endless succession of other doll-related items: dishes, furniture, animals and a whole slew of other things. I also save plastic baby wipe containers (the ones that look like huge Lego

47

blocks) to store the even-smaller things such as Barbie shoes, purses, hangers, brushes and other mini-accessories that seem to come with all dolls these days. Plastic shoe boxes and lunch meat containers are other options you can have for storing small items.

Yes, you'll still spend a great deal of time picking up and putting away every item in the playroom – over and over! But you can actually use this time for more than just cleaning up. Think of it as an opportunity to go through the toys and stuffed animals, and only keep the ones that your children still play with – and that are complete and are still in good shape.

Art supplies: Here s an especially useful item: a wooden three-level rack that holds different sizes and color plastic bins, lying at an angle. It can be found at stores such as Target, Meijer's, Wal-Mart, Kmart and other such stores, and it is particularly useful for storing art supplies:

- Construction paper
- Coloring books
- Crayons, markers
- Scissors
- Paint brushes
- Stickers
- And all the other things your kids accumulate to make their one of a kind crafts.

Display it too. And don't just store all that lovely art. Hang their handiwork on the playroom walls and make it your kids' own unique space. If you can get a bulletin board or a corkboard, that s great, or you can simply string rope or twine from one end of the space to the other and hang the art with clothespins or paperclips. I have also purchased clipboards made of glass or plastic and used those to post their art in other areas around the house like near the back door or garage door entry. You can even display the larger and better pieces in inexpensive frames; using colored construction paper as a matte to fill in the space (we know the art never exactly fits the frame, does it?). It looks very nice, and your child will be so proud.

Stuffed animals: They seem to have a mind of their own, but I have found that a big open bin or laundry basket is perfect for storing stuffed animals. Yes, picking them up and giving them a home is a never-ending job, but here, too, you can use this time to go through and eliminate the old, broken, and used once.

Toy boxes: You can stack the boxes on top of one another against the wall. This way when they are looking to play with the Build-A-Bears, Lego s or Baby Dolls, they can pull just pull the box and they have everything.

Yes, you'll still spend a great deal of time picking up and putting away every item in the playroom over and over! But you can actually use this time for more than just cleaning up. Think of it as an opportunity to go through the toys and stuffed animals, and only keep the ones that your children still play with and that are complete and in good shape. I actually try and clean out the toy room when the kids are not home. Of course, you know what their favorite's toys are: usually the ones that are in excellent shape can be eliminated because they are the toys they hardly ever play with. These can be sold or given away to someone who will enjoy them.

Where to find the best storage containers? The big box" stores like Target and Wal-Mart are always good, but don't overlook the art supply and hardware stores either like: Michaels, Hobby Lobby, Lowes, Home Depot and others in your area.

Office

An organized office will make your life run efficiently. You'll be amazed. First go through you drawers and take a look at how you have them organized. Do you have receipts and bills from 3 years ago along with a 2 year old birthday card? Let us clean it out.

Set up your file drawers:
- Monthly bills
- Utility bills
- Banking (a file for each bank along with checking, saving, CD, IRA s) and any other investments.
- A household file which has the home repairs and services in this area. Medical files
- School, lessons
- Income tax (file the items you will need for filling taxes. Donations, property tax, bank statements, last year's tax statement, etc.)
- Household warranties
- And the hundreds of other warranties we receive. I make them up into files of their own.
- Kitchen
- Outdoors
- Household items small and large

This makes it easier to locate the warranties when

needed instead of having to search through all of them. Also there are so many of them that you can look at and get rid of. Do you really need the warranty on the $12.95 alarm clock? These can also be stored in a storage box if you run out of file drawers.

You can go to an office supply store and purchase storage boxes. Use them to store your:

- Tax Returns
- Bank Statements
- Charge Account Bills
- Medical Bills
- School Records

These file boxes can be stored in your storage area can t forget to label the boxes as this will make it much easier to find things if and when they are needed.

Look at all the pens, pencils and desk supplies you have and put them in the area where they will be used. Keep them in the same spot, this way they are easy to find.

Another thing I have done is purchase a card box. I don t know about you, but I love cards. I always go to the card section and read the cards. Some I buy just because I think they are hilarious and others I see and it reminds me of a certain someone that fits the card. I have a file and I put it in the section that says birthday, sympathy, get well, whatever cards I have. You never know when you hear of a sickness or a death and want to send a card but by the time you get to the store it is after the fact. It's so nice to have them on hand for emergencies.

I also write in my calendar the people who I would send a card to I mark their birthdays this way it reminds me to send a card.

I also try and organize my photos. I know this is an endless job. I'm still not finished with mine, thank goodness for the digital camera. I can know just store them on a disk and file that. The thing now is to label and date each disk so that they are easier to locate when needed.

Storage Room

This is a big area to cover because we store sooo many things.

Luggage: I don't know how often you travel but if it's weekly/monthly on business or every other weekend sending the kids to the other parent's house, whatever the case may be you know what pieces to have at the front spot. The luggage that is less frequently used can be stored under the stairs, in the garage, in the attic, or in the back of the store room. I have a large plastic container 32" x 15" x 13' that I store all the extra small bags in. Take a look at the luggage you have do you use it all or can you eliminate some of the smaller extra bags that you have received over the years you know the extra bags you get for free with the purchase at the make-up counter. Do you really use or need them?

Holiday Decorations: I buy the large 32" x 15" x 13' sterilized containers from most stores. I like the ones that are clear so you can see what is in the container. These are also easy to stack. I know this may seem like an expense you don't need so why not just use the boxes that they came in? I have found that if you buy the same boxes to store all the decorations in then it saves on space. They can be stacked on top of one another and the area is much neater and not so overwhelming. You can buy bubble wrap in large rolls from most office supply stores and wrap the decorations to store. Some will need bigger bins and maybe more than one while others may only need one small bin. Whatever the sizes are, buy the same sized small and large bins so they are easy to stack on one another.

Christmas Decorations: A box that holds the tree decorations one or two that hold the room decorations. You know what you have and you can group them by the room and area they will be going in. Some can fit it all in one bin and others (like me) need about 8 of them.

Think about the holidays you have decorations for, start in January and work your way through the year. New Years, Valentines, St Patrick's, Spring, Easter, 4th of July, Halloween, Autumn, Winter, Christmas/ Hanukkah/Kwanza, Birthdays and any other celebration you have decorations for.
Then if you have room in the storage area or garage to hold the larger decorative items such as the Santa in his sleigh, decorative holiday flags and all the other holiday decorations. Try and put them in a container. But I know that some are larger than others and that they cannot be stored in a container. Then you could take a large leaf bag and wrap the items up and stand it on its own. You know what you have and do what you can.

Wrapping supplies: I have a rack that I put the long thin plastic bin to hold the large bows and boxes in and then I have a hanging rack that I hang large bags which hold the gift bags in, one for extra bags another for Christmas, Birthdays, fun all occasion bags, and all else you have purchased. Under the rod I have a large plastic bin that holds the wrapping paper I also use the plastic 3 drawers on wheels to hold the bows, ribbons, tape, scissors and tags in.

Party favors: Favors from year to year. When you have a birthday party, New Year or any other Holiday celebration and buy all the party favors such as banners, signs and centerpieces, hats, etc. These items can be used for another celebration. I have a Happy Birthday banner that I bought, I can't even remember how long ago, but I still hang it up with balloons so the Birthday person has a fun way to start off their day. I know you don't use up all of the napkins, plates and cups so keep the leftovers and you will have some for the next celebration. I realize that you can't do this when you are having a party but unless you have a big celebration for everyone's birthday you can use them again for the family dinner or lunch. There even fun to send packed in your child's lunch if they have their Birthday on a school day. I usually buy the birthday cakes so they do have plastic decorations on the cake which I wash off and keep in a plastic tub. If I do make a birthday cake I may be able to use them again, if all else fails, my daughter has fun making cupcakes and decorating them.

Fragile items: An office supply store will carry a big

roll of the bubble wrap. I would suggest getting this and storing the dishes, glassware and any other figurines wrapped in this. This will let you get rid of the boxes that take up to much space. Store them in the same bin. Don't put them in with other items that take up room and may damage the items. You know the items that you store in your storage area each household is different but I suggest that you take a look at all that you store and ask yourself if you really need to hold onto it? Do you have large parties that you need all those extra dishes and glassware? When was the last time you used these items? And is there a time that will come up when you would you use them again? You could probably get rid of a majority of items from old luggage, clothing, dishware, toys, knickknacks, tools and anything else you store that you don't use. Yes there are items that have sentimental value to and you can't part with. So, clean it up and put it out to display, or put these things in a fresh storage container that you can set aside in the back of the store room. You need to label them, of course.

Garage/Shed

I realize that every area is different. It's best to first empty out the garage; yes I realize that this will be a much bigger task for some but you need to clear it all out. This is obviously a job to be done on a nice clear and dry day. Once the garage is empty you need to sweep all the dirt off the floor and then hose it down. You are probably thinking AHHH!!! What do I do now?

Again look at what you are storing in the garage. Can it go in the house anywhere; can you get rid of it? Do like what you did in the storage room. If you have items that can be put in the bins (I mean storage or trash) then do so.

You probably have larger items such as:

- Lawn mowers
- Snow plows
- Fertilizer spreaders

Store the items that you use for the season in the front and the items you don't use in the back. You don t need to get to the snow plow in July or the lawn mower in December.

You can purchase some hooks from the home supply store and hang up the following:

- Rakes
- Brooms

- Shovels
- Hoses

and all the other items that you have leaning in the corner of the garage.

Might I suggest getting the large hooks to hang your bikes on, I realize that if its nice weather and you ride them often then this is not a good idea but you can store them during the winter when you're not riding them.

The outdoor items are what you need to store in the garage or shed.

Some may also have their work bench with all the tools out in the garage. You need to designate an area for this with either a work bench or a storage shed, which you can get from any home hardware store. Again you need to organize this area too.

Get the storage bins that are in the tool area of the store or you can even use:

- Old shoe boxes
- Butter tubs
- Coffee cans
- Food jars

These can be used to store your bolts, nails and screws in.

I like to use the plastic baskets that come in a variety of sizes to store things such as:

- Extension cords
- Ropes
- Tape measures
- Protective glasses, gloves
- The list goes on and on

Look at what you have and what you use and you can get organized.

Another item you can store in the garage is the outdoor holiday decorations. Get a large bin to store the lights, snowmen and candy canes in and put it in a corner or the attic of the garage. And of course, you need to have waste bins.

Conclusion

I can't stress this enough. Only store the items in the area they are used. This eliminates thing getting lost and it also eliminates clutter.

You will be amazed at how you will feel with having a well organized house. This will eliminate clutter, waste and stress.

Once you get the area finished and you work it for a while if it s not working the way you want, you can tweak it to what will work for you.

I know that every home and situation is different but I hope this will give you some ideas on how to organize your space. If you have any questions or if there is an area I have not covered, you can send me a message on my blog and I will respond to your questions within 48 hours.

My blog is http://help-organize.blogspot.com/

Where To Buy Websites

www.acehardware.com/
www.acohardware.com/
www.bedbathandbeyond.com
www.containerstore.com
www.dollargeneral.com/
www.hobbylobby.com
www.homedepot.com/
www.kmart.com/
www.lowes.com
www.meijer.com
www.menards.com/
www.michaels.com
www.officemax.com/
www.sears.com/
www.staples.com/
www.target.com/
www.truevalue.com/
www.walmart.com
www.rubbermaid.com
www.OfficeDepot.com
www.ReallyGoodStuff.com/Organizers
www.craftamerica.com/storage_containers.htm

Printed in Great Britain
by Amazon.co.uk, Ltd.,
Marston Gate.